HOW TO CHANGE YOUR FINANCIAL MINDSET:

A 10-STEP GUIDED JOURNAL FOR SUCCESS

How To Change Your Financial Mindset: A 10-Step Guided Journal For Success

For permission requests, please contact the publisher by email at:
support@wisemindsshop.org

Identifier: ISBN: 978-1-966514-20-6 (paperback)

Published by: Wise Minds

First Edition

Printed in the United States of America

ABOUT THE GUIDE

In today's economy, it can feel impossible to catch a break, let alone thrive. However, we believe that with the right mindset, steps, and habits, you can not only survive—you can build wealth to thrive. This guide is designed to help make that process easier.

Inside, you'll find:

- 10 Actionable steps to transform your financial mindset.
- "What to Do" prompts to keep you on track.
- "Why It Matters" explanations to help you digest the importance of each step.
- "Food For Thought" quotes & visuals to ponder on.
- Reflection questions to help you dig deeper and explore your understanding of each prompt.

- & A BONUS STEP!

MESSAGE FROM THE AUTHOR

Hey friend!

We know how frustrating it can be to feel stuck, unsure, and overwhelmed when it comes to your money. Understand that **you've already taken the first step** to financial peace by opening this guide. That means you're ready for change & it's beginning now.

We've been stuck before, just like everyone else. In this guide, you'll find the same principles we used to break ourselves out of financial survival mode.

We believe anyone can do this; you just need the right mindset. We can't wait for you to **see what's possible when you embrace change**. You can only grow from here, remember that.

YOU GOT THIS FRIEND!

Wise Minds

HOW TO USE THIS GUIDE

This guide is designed to help you break free from limiting beliefs and build the financial future you deserve. Here's how to make the most of it:

- **Take Your Time:** Each step is meant to be deeply reflective, so don't rush through it! Give yourself the space to truly ponder and explore each section. Completing the guide in a week or even a month may not be enough time for the lessons to stick.

- **Follow Your Pace:** There's no set timeline for this guide. Move forward only when you feel ready and confident in your progress. Some steps may take longer than others—and that's okay!

- **Make It Personal:** This guide isn't just about reading; it's about ACTION. It's highly recommended that you use the journal pages to complete the "What to Do" & "Reflection Questions" sections to apply what you're learning to your own life. Be intentional with this tool.

- **Stay Consistent:** Revisiting your reflections and building habits along the way will help cement your growth.

- **Enjoy the Journey:** This is a time to invest in yourself and your future. Celebrate every small win as you grow into the person who will achieve their most desired goals!

STEP 1: REFLECT ON YOUR MONEY STORY

What to Do:

- Identify your earliest memories and feelings about money.
- Were they positive, negative, or a mix? Write down any beliefs you inherited about money (i.e. "You have to work hard to be rich").

Why It Matters:

- Your relationship with money often stems from early to late childhood.
- Understanding your “money story” helps you uncover limiting beliefs and where they came from.

STEP 1: REFLECT ON YOUR MONEY STORY

Food for Thought:

Money is a tool and my beliefs about it will continue to change.

Reflection Questions:

- What have you learned?
- How has your past shaped the way you view money today?
- What did you discover about your money story that surprised you the most?
- What beliefs about money are serving you positively?

MONEY IS A TOOL
& MY FEELINGS TOWARD IT WILL
CHANGE

STEP 2: REDEFINE WHAT WEALTH MEANS TO YOU

What to Do:

- List 3-5 non-material things that make you feel rich (i.e. family, love, etc.).
- Then, redefine wealth in a way that aligns with your values (i.e., "Wealth means having the freedom to spend time with loved ones without financial stress").

Why It Matters:

- Redefining wealth is the key to your success in shifting your financial mindset.
- When you connect money to your core values, you approach it with purpose.

Food for Thought:

True wealth is financial freedom, not possessions.

Reflection Questions:

- What have you learned?
- In what ways does your current definition of wealth align with your values?
- What was the most meaningful non-material thing on your list, and why?

TRUE WEALTH IS

FINANCIAL FREEDOM

NOT POSSESSIONS

STEP 3: PRACTICE GRATITUDE FOR WHAT YOU HAVE

What to Do:

- Write down three or more things you're grateful for that money couldn't buy and one thing you're grateful for that money did provide (i.e., family, groceries, etc.).

Why It Matters:

- Gratitude rewires your brain to focus on abundance rather than lack, while reducing feelings of stress or envy and creating feelings of happiness or peace.

- Practicing gratitude helps you recognize the wealth already present in your life.

STEP 3: PRACTICE GRATITUDE FOR WHAT YOU HAVE

Food for Thought:

I am already successful & rich in my own abundance.

Reflection Questions:

- What have you learned?
- How has being thankful changed the way you think about what it means to be rich?
- What is one way you can regularly remind yourself of the good things in your life?
- How can practicing gratitude daily improve your financial decisions?

I AM ALREADY

SUCCESSFUL & RICH

IN MY OWN ABUNDANCE

STEP 4: DETACH FROM SOCIETAL PRESSURE

What to Do:

- Reflect on societal norms that influence how you spend or feel about money (i.e., salary comparison, trendy or designer fashion, etc.).
- Decide which of these norms you'll reject moving forward & stand on it!

Why It Matters:

- It's possible some norms may be the root cause of your unhealthy money habits.
- Society often equates success with materialism, but this can lead to financial stress and dissatisfaction in life overall.

Food for Thought:

My worth is not defined by what I own or spend.

Reflection Questions:

- What have you learned?
- How can you apply what you learned today to make a real change in your financial behavior?
- What's one societal norm that's a non-negotiable for you?
- What's one that you've followed before that you've never agreed with?

my WORTH

IS NOT

DEFINED BY

MY SALARY

STEP 5: SHIFT FROM SCARCITY TO ABUNDANCE THINKING

What to Do:

- When you feel tempted to say, "I can't afford that," quickly reframe it as, "How can I afford that?".
- List ways to create opportunities for yourself (i.e., side hustles, networking, etc.).

Why It Matters:

- Scarcity mindsets produce lots of limiting thoughts, which leads to limited behavior and stumps your growth.
- While abundance mindsets produce possibilities, while continuously seeking more possibilities.

Food for Thought:

- A scarcity mindset will NEVER have the opportunity to turn ideas into plans.
- When I focus on possibilities, I unlock the power to create the future I desire.

Reflection Questions:

- What have you learned?
- What opportunities can you create today that move you closer to abundance?

WHEN I FOCUS ON ***POSSIBILITIES***

I UNLOCK THE POWER TO ***CREATE***

THE FUTURE I ***DESIRE***

STEP 6: COMMIT TO A CLEAR FINANCIAL VISION

What to Do:

- Write a detailed vision of your ideal financial life. Be specific (i.e., "I will pay off my credit card debt next year", "I will save $____").
- Break this vision into small, actionable goals (i.e. I can make my favorite iced coffee drink at home and pay myself $7 every time.).

Why It Matters:

- A detailed vision provides clarity and inspiration while keeping your goals at the forefront.
- Without a vision, it's easy to lose focus or give up when challenges arise.

Food for Thought:

Every decision I make today either brings me closer to or further from my vision.

Reflection Questions:

- What have you learned?
- What is the most inspiring or fulfilling part of your financial vision?
- What roadblocks might you face, and how will you break through them?
- How will achieving your financial vision impact your relationships, career, and lifestyle?

EVERY DECISION I MAKE TODAY

EITHER BRINGS ME CLOSER TO

OR FURTHER FROM MY

VISION

STEP 7: EMBRACE THE POWER OF CONSISTENCY

What to Do:

- Automate savings, set recurring payments for debts, or commit to daily habits like tracking spending.
- Start small to avoid overwhelming feelings. Consider withdrawing your weekly lunch expense in cash or using specific cards for specific purposes like gas and groceries.

Why It Matters:

- Consistency compounds over time, turning small actions into major results whether that's with interest or building healthy habits.

Food for Thought

Small, steady steps create lasting wins.

Reflection Questions:

- What have you learned?
- What's one financial habit you've already nailed, and how does that make you feel?
- What's one area where consistency could improve your financial mindset?
- If you stayed consistent for the next 6 months, what changes would you expect to see?

Food for Thought:

Small, steady steps create lasting wins.

Reflection Questions:

- What have you learned?
- What's one financial habit you've already nailed, and how does that make you feel?
- What's one area where consistency could improve your financial mindset?
- If you stayed consistent for the next 3-6 months, what changes would you expect to see?

PHONE
KEEP GOING!
SMALL STEADY STEPS CREATE
LASTING WINS

STEP 8: REFRAME SETBACKS AS LEARNING OPPORTUNITIES

What to Do:

- Write down some financial mistakes you've made and list 3-5 lessons you learned from them all.
- Take note of any patterns you see or remember about your financial mistakes. Lean into why you made the decision(s) in the first place.

Why It Matters:

- Mistakes are inevitable, but they will guide smarter decisions moving forward if & only if you choose to learn from them.

STEP 8: REFRAME SETBACKS AS LEARNING OPPORTUNITIES

Food for Thought:

Mistakes and challenges help us grow in character and success.

Reflection Questions:

- How can you turn lessons from past mistakes into opportunities for growth?
- What would you tell your past self about overcoming your financial barriers?
- What steps will you take to reinforce the positive habits you're building this week?
- What's one mistake you're now grateful for because of the lesson it taught you?

CHALLENGES HELP US GROW
MISTAKES HELP US GROW
CHALLENGES HELP US GROW
MISTAKES HELP US GROW
CHALLENGES HELP US GROW
MISTAKES HELP US GROW
CHALLENGES HELP US GROW
MISTAKES HELP US GROW
MISTAKES HELP US GROW
CHALLENGES HELP US GROW
MISTAKES HELP US GROW

STEP 9: FOCUS ON BUILDING WEALTH, NOT JUST MAKING MONEY!

What to Do:

- Look into passive income opportunities, investments, or skills that increase your earning potential.
- Commit to long-term strategies rather than get-rich-quick schemes.

Why It Matters:

- Building wealth creates stability and freedom, while side hustles & quick income can lead to burnout.
- Wealth focuses on long-term growth and sustainability, giving you options no matter what life throws at you.
- Learning wealth-building strategies can help break cycles of financial stress for you and future generations.

Food for Thought:

Remember you can only lower your expenses so much, especially with inflation...

However, your earning potential will always remain the same: UNLIMITED.

Invest in your mind. The more you learn, the more you'll earn.

Reflection Questions:

- What steps can you take to turn your passions or skills into a source of wealth?
- How can you focus on building something today that benefits you 5–10 years from now?
- What's one area of wealth-building or passive income you'd like to learn more about?

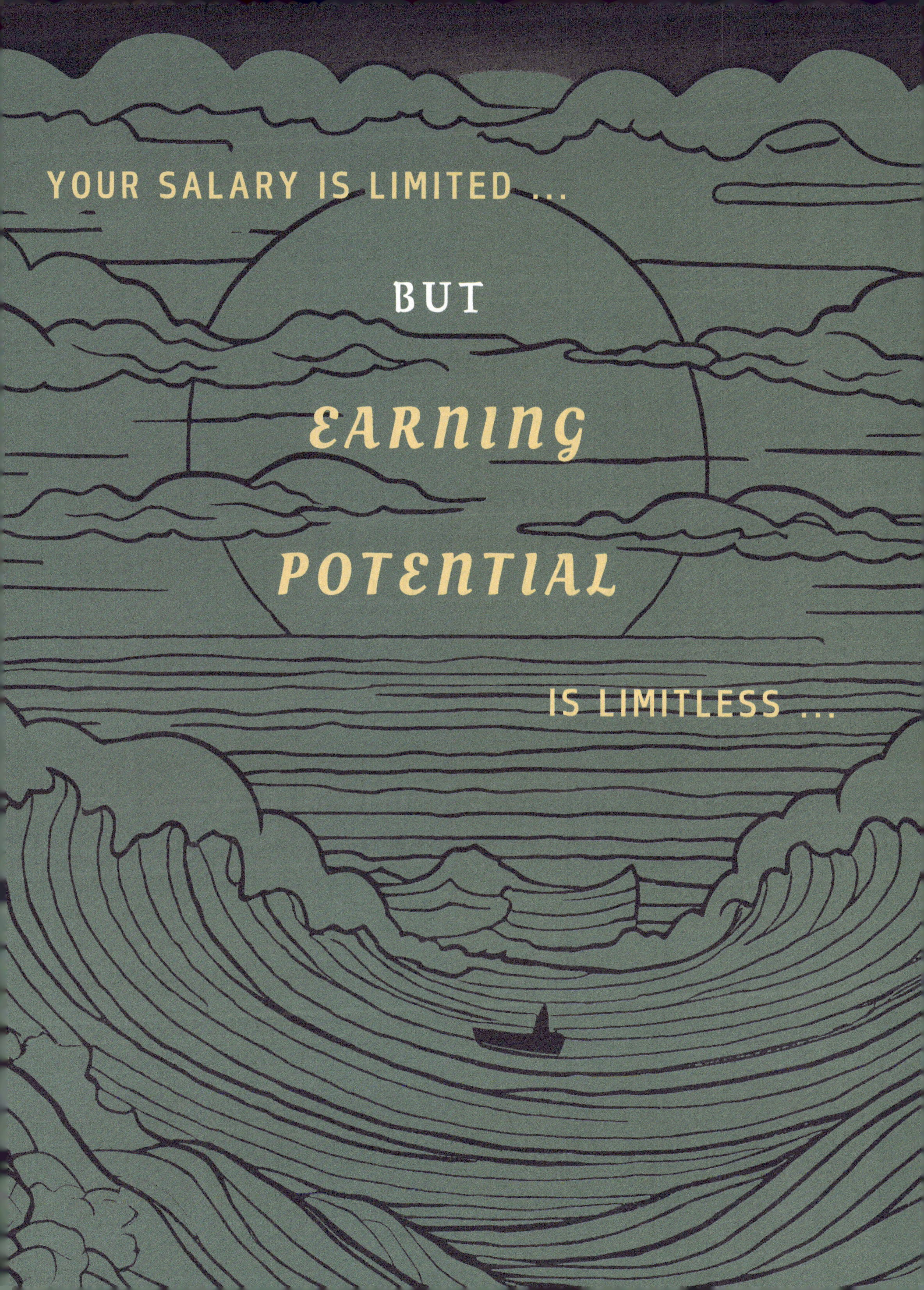
YOUR SALARY IS LIMITED ...
BUT
EARNING
POTENTIAL
IS LIMITLESS ...

STEP 10: GIVE GENEROUSLY WITHOUT FEAR

What to Do:

- Donate a small, intentional amount to a cause you want to see grow.
- Try a small organization like that guy you see on social media that serves the homeless warm meals when he can afford to.

Why It Matters:

- Generosity reminds you that there's always more than enough, adding to your abundant mindset.
- Generosity creates a ripple effect. Your small act of kindness can inspire others to give, too!
- Generosity isn't just about money—your time, skills, or kind words can spark joy and create meaningful change.

Food for Thought:

We create the futures we want to see by making change today.

Reflection Questions:

- What cause did you donate to?
- What did your donation equate to for someone else?
- How else can you help the cause grow? (Remember, social media is a free resource!)
- How did giving to this cause make you feel?

TOMORROW
DONATION
WE CREATE
THE FUTURES
WE WANT
TO SEE!

BONUS STEP: CELEBRATE YOUR WINS!

What to Do:

- Think back to when you first purchased this guide & how different you think about money now!

- List any financial milestones you've met & celebrate in a way that's meaningful to you!

- Appreciate how far you've come, continue turning away from your unhealthy money habits, and keep pushing forward!

Why It Matters:

- Celebrating progress reinforces positive habits and keeps you motivated.

- It also tricks your brain to like discipline.

BONUS STEP: CELEBRATE YOUR WINS!

Food for Thought:

Every step forward is worth celebrating, no matter the size of the step!

Reflection Questions:

- What was the hardest part of this journey/challenge?
- What did you enjoy most?
- How can you continue to move forward?

Join the Conversation!

Visit the Wise Minds Chat Groups at www.WiseMindsShop.org to share your wins, celebrate your progress, and connect with others on the same journey!

We'd love to hear your thoughts about this guide! Please email us at support@wisemindsshop.org

KEEP MOVING
FORWARD!

AFFIRMATIONS & PLACES TO DONATE

Affirmations to Takeaway:

- I AM capable of building wealth.
- I AM able to attract opportunities that align with my values and dreams.
- I AM grateful for the abundance already present in my life.
- I AM breaking generational barriers and creating new cycles of success for myself & my family.

Small Organizations That Make A Huge Impact:

- <u>Made to Serve:</u> A non-profit organization graciously serving the homeless in Austin, TX.
    - www.madetoserve.org
- <u>New Jersey Film Academy:</u> An organization committed to bridging the gap between education and employment in the film and media industry.
    - www.njfilmacademy.org
- <u>Cross Bridge Community Church:</u> Hosts an annual prom for young individuals with special needs.
    - www.crossbridgecc.org

END OF CHALLENGE

Congratulations on completing the How to Change your Financial Mindset Challenge!

By taking this time to reshape your financial mindset, you've set yourself up for lasting success.

Congrats on taking this major step, embracing progress and building the life you truly desire!

@WiseMindsLLC

www.WiseMindsShop.org

Made in the USA
Monee, IL
02 November 2026

67387594R00044